TopReaders

Animals at Home

Denise Ryan

Contents

There are many wild places
on Earth. Let's visit
some of them.

Grasslands

Zebras and giraffes live in Africa's grasslands.

zebra

giraffe

Grasslands have grass,
a few trees, and low shrubs.

Deserts

Deserts are places where
it hardly ever rains.
Sandy deserts are hot and dry.

water-storing tree

Desert plants store water
in their leaves, branches, or trunks.

sharp peak

Mountains

Mountains are high places.
Some have sharp peaks.

People sometimes grow crops on the sides of mountains.

Rain Forests

Rain forests are thick, warm, and wet forests.

rain forest trees and vines

Plants grow well in rain forests because they get a lot of rain!

Evergreen Forests

Some cold forests have trees
that stay green all year.

Mammals and birds live
in these cold forests.

yellow leaves

orange leaves

Forests in Autumn

Trees that grow in some forests lose their leaves each year.

autumn leaves

In autumn, the leaves turn red, orange, and yellow. Then they drop off the trees.

Ponds

Ponds are small, quiet places that have fresh water.

rushes

water lily

Water lilies grow in the water and rushes grow on the banks.

Rock Pools

Rock pools are pools of salty water on the edge of the sea.

Lots of different sea creatures
find homes in a rock pool.

Islands

Islands are pieces of land
with water all around them.
Some are tiny, but others
are large.

crab

iguana

Iguanas, penguins, crabs, and seals
live on this island.

penguin

seal

Arctic Tundra

The Arctic tundra is a wild place where the ground is always frozen.

In summer, beautiful flowers bloom for a very short time.

Quiz

Can you match each plant with its name?

autumn leaves   water-storing tree

rain forest trees   water lily